Foreword

I am deeply thankful to my friend Ron Clark for his counsel. His many calls and prayers have encouraged me to complete this book. Also, Coby Ringgenberg who helped me with the book cover and who posted the GoFundMe page. Her efforts were tops.

God's deep impressions, by His Holy Spirit drove me on in writing the outline and woke me up in the late night and early mornings to write this book while in the hospital. I was blessed by my God to help me write this book-my first book to His glory.

It is my prayer that all who read this small but powerful book will be blessed and saved for the soon return of our Lord Jesus.

God bless you all,
Bruce Atchison

Facing Today and Beyond

Bruce Atchison

TEACH Services, Inc.
PUBLISHING
www.TEACHServices.com • (800) 367-1844

Copyright © 2021 Bruce Atchison
Copyright © 2021 TEACH Services, Inc.
ISBN-13: 978-1-4796-1300-7 (Paperback)

All Bible text references are taken from the King James Version (KJV) of the Bible unless otherwise stated. Public domain.

Bible references labeled (NIV) are taken from the Holy Bible, New International Version®, NIV® Copyright ©1973, 1978, 1984, 2011 by Biblica, Inc.® Used by permission. All rights reserved worldwide.

Bible references labeld (NKJV) are taken from the New King James Version®. Copyright © 1982 by Thomas Nelson. Used by permission. All rights reserved.

We invite you to view the complete selection of titles we publish at
www.TEACHServices.com

TEACH Services' titles may be purchased in bulk quantities for educational, fundraising, business, or promotional use. Write to **bulksales@TEACHServices.com**

If you are interested in seeing your own book in print, please contact us at
publishing@TEACHServices.com

Published by

TEACH Services, Inc.
P U B L I S H I N G
www.TEACHServices.com • (800) 367-1844

Table of Contents

Introduction. 4

Chapter 1 4

   a. History of Our Health Practices in America from
      1800 and Beyond 4

   b. Special Laws of Health Given to Us by God 5

   c. Further History of Health and the Black Plague
      (1348–1351) 6

   d. Lifestyle Principles for Today 7

   e. Health Worksheet 12

Chapter 2 13

   a. Facing Life's Trials 13

   b. Trial Illustration 14

   c. How Can Trials Benefit Us? 14

   d. Future World Problems—Our Life Trials 15

   e. Trials Worksheet 17

Chapter 3 18

   a. Intercessory Prayer 18

   b. How Prayer Works 20

   c. Prayer Worksheet 21

Book Summary 22

Super Foods to Keep One in Optimal Health 22

Boosting Your Immune System the NEW START Way
by Barbara Watson Paille 23

Introduction

To all my friends who are struggling to make sense of the current world troubles—be it COVID-19 or any other world issues—may you be blessed by reading what God has given me to share with you. This book delves into the health history of our beloved country, America, and touches on health issues elsewhere. The perspectives of this book are presented as principles from which we all can learn and are here recorded to aid you in your journey to optimal health in the *physical*, *mental,* and *spiritual* realms.

Chapter 1

History of Our Health Practices in America from 1800 and Beyond

When I was a young boy the "Wild West" appealed to me. To have a six-shooter revolver in my hand and a cigar in my mouth were my desire. Drinking alcohol went along with this lifestyle (not exactly what we want our children to be watching!). I wanted to be like these Wild West heroes so much that the likes of TV programs such as Gunsmoke and Bonanza were a must to watch each week to live out my dreams. These programs captivated my total attention and lived on even into my tour in the US Air Force during the Vietnam War.

Question … where these days really the ones that you would have liked to have lived in? Death came early. The average life expectancy in 1860 was only 39.4 years![1] Today a person can expect to live to the ripe-old age of 78.6 years[2]—very nearly double that of a person in the Wild West.

The following notes are taken from the book *Legacy* by Richard H. Schaefer. Tuberculosis (TB, a disease of the lungs) killed many, even young adults in their early 20s. The American Medical Association (AMA), which started in 1847, would not even be recognizable if compared to the AMA of today. How our medical standards have changed!

Some examples from the 1800s to around 1900 will suffice to illustrate how different things were a century ago.

---

[1]"Life Expectancy (from Birth) in the United States, from 1860 to 2020," https://1ref.us/1bu (accessed Jun. 24, 2020).

[2]CDC, "FastStats—Life Expectancy," https://1ref.us/1bv (accessed Jun. 24, 2020).

1. *Typhoid fever* was a common ailment that was spread through contaminated food or water or in close contact with an infected person.[3] The treatment? Let the patient have no fresh air or cold water and they were given poisonous drugs such as calomel, opium, heroin, mercury, arsenic, and strychnine.
2. *Strokes*, while still common today, were treated by draining one's blood.[4]
3. *Tobacco*, which we know today causes problems like lung cancer, circulatory issues, and high blood pressure, was once recommended treatment for any lung ailment.[5]
4. *Traditional Native American remedies* included tonics of alcohol and opium (a highly-addictive narcotic drug).
5. *Earaches* were often treated by blowing smoke into the inner ear.
6. The *common cold* has no known cure even today, but back then patients were told to mix together 1 teaspoon each of sugar, mineral oil, and ginger, the juice of 1 lemon, and 2 ounces of 100% whiskey.[6]
7. Even our first president, George Washington, could not escape the *curse of un-enlightened medicine*. Upon contracting a throat infection,[7] he was bled to death.[8] Bloodletting was a common treatment for many illnesses.[9]

But this form of misguided medicine was not all bad. Miraculously some good also prevailed such as:

1. Dr. Larkin B. Coles, a health reformer who advocated a proper diet and regular meals "opposed the use of tobacco and all narcotics."[10]
2. Dr. James C. Jackson, a forward-thinking physician in New York, in 1858 prescribed water treatments like hot and cold showers and encouraged wholesome diet.[11]

Special Laws of Health Given to Us by God

Medicine was not all bad, but overall medical treatments were very much lacking. Into this sad medical environment came God's help.

---

[3]Mayo Clinic, "Typhoid Fever," https://1ref.us/1bw (accessed Jun. 28, 2020).
[4]Richard H. Schaefer, *Legacy* (Mountain View, CA: Pacific Press, 1977), p. 4.
[5]Richard H. Schaefer, *Legacy* (Mountain View, CA: Pacific Press, 1977), p. 7.
[6]Richard H. Schaefer, *Legacy* (Mountain View, CA: Pacific Press, 1977), p. 10.
[7]MountVernon.Org, "8 Facts About the Death of George Washington," https://1ref.us/1bx (accessed Jun. 28, 2020).
[8]Richard H. Schaefer, *Legacy* (Mountain View, CA: Pacific Press, 1977), p. 3.
[9]*British Columbia Medical Journal,* "The History of Bloodletting," https://1ref.us/1by (accessed Jun. 28, 2020).
[10]Richard H. Schaefer, *Legacy* (Mountain View, CA: Pacific Press, 1977), p. 12.
[11]Loma Linda University, https://1ref.us/1bz (accessed Jun. 28, 2020).

In 1863 the Seventh-day Adventist Church had about 3,500 church members. One prominent member was Ellen G. White. Her 1863 health vision spoke of the need to implement the principles of the original diet that God gave Adam and Eve in the Garden of Eden. She also addressed the natural remedies and lifestyle practices designed by our Creator to give mankind optimal health.

In the 1870s and beyond Dr. John Harvey Kellogg implemented natural healing techniques and a return to God's original diet. Dr. Kellogg, of Kellogg's Corn Flakes, helped build the largest hospital in the world at the time—the Battle Creek Sanitarium. Even President Taft, Warren G. Harding, and other world leaders and famous people of the era went there to be treated.[12]

Further, in 1909 Ellen G. White wrote a book called *The Ministry in Healing*. In this book she elaborated on God's health laws and natural healing remedies all designed to boost our immune system and live an optimal health life. This would include physical, mental, and spiritual health. Some high points of this book include:[13]

1. Diseases are caused by violating God's health laws.
2. Recovery will be blessed by following God's health laws in the Old Testament of the Bible. Such elements include good nutrition, water, sunlight, temperance, and trust in God.

Further History of Health and the Black Plague (1347–1351)

Before I go into detail on each point listed above it would do us all good to see how not following these health principles worked in the world's history. Specifically, we will take a look at the Black Plague in Europe between 1347 and 1351. This plague was Europe's deadliest pandemic in history (also known as the Bubonic Plague or Black Plague).[14]

This plague struck Europe because of unsanitary conditions, crowded towns, and the basic living conditions of the poorer classes. Streets were undrained and this helped spread leprosy and fever as well. The death toll for this pandemic was up to 50 million lives in Europe (about 60% of the population) and even more world-wide.[15] What was ultimately the cause? Fleas on rats. It took 200 years for Europe's population to recover.[16]

---

[12]"Battle Creek Sanitarium," Wikipedia, https://1ref.us/1c0 (accessed Jun. 28, 2020).
[13]Ellen G. White, *The Ministry of Healing¸* chapter 17, "The Use of Remedies" (Mountain View, CA: Pacific Press Publishing Association, 1905).
[14]"How 5 of History's Worst Pandemics Finally Ended," History Channel, https://1ref.us/1c1 (accessed Jun. 28, 2020).
[15]"The Black Death: The Greatest Catastrophe Ever," *History Today,* https://1ref.us/1c2 (accessed Jun. 28, 2020).
[16]"Black Death," Ancient History Encyclopedia, https://1ref.us/1c3 (accessed Jun. 28, 2020).

Eventually God's health laws were practiced by some. One of these practices was quarantine (Lev. 13:2) for an initial seven days if a person was suspected of having leprosy. If leprosy was found a total separation from society was their lot until the virus ran its course or death occurred. In addition, washing clothes and regular baths (Num.19:5) as well as wearing clean clothes (Exod. 19:5) was implemented by some.

A striking example of the power of health and sanitation occurred during the Black Plague. At this time the Jewish people were forced to live in ghettoes away from the Gentiles and only left the ghetto at their own peril. A distinguished Jewish physician, Balavignus, encouraged the people in his ghetto to implement the sanitation laws found in Leviticus. "Balavignus was also a master of Jewish tradition and was in a position to apply literally the principles of Pentateuchal sanitation. These writings of Moses contain most practical instructions relating to disinfection and the incineration of refuse. The laws of health laid down in Leviticus are the basis of moderen sanitary science."[17] They burned all of the refuse, covered their wells and took away buckets that could breed sickness. Ultimately the mortality rate in the Jewish ghetto was only five percent of what it was in neighboring Gentile areas! While today we know that is a result of sanitary living, in 1346 the non-Jewish people were highly superstitious and believed the Jews were poisoning them, leading to angry Gentile mobs and a general massacre of the Jewish people.[18]

So, what finally led to the end of the "Black Death"? According to David Riesman, professor of the History of Medicine at the University of Pennsylvania: "Isolation of the sick and quarantine came into use. These practices not only eliminated the plague as a pandemic menace for the first time in history but also led to general laws against infectious diseases, thereby laying the foundations upon which modern hygiene rests."[19]

Lifestyle Principles for Today

Now let's look at an acronym, NEWSTART, by the Weimar Institute in California. Also known as the eight laws of health, each letter in this acronym represents a very important element in the health of the whole person. A great and accessible resource to learn more about these laws is a video called "8 Laws to a Better, Longer Life."[20] Going hand in hand with this video is a booklet called "Light Up Your Life: Learn How to Live

---

[17]Atkinson, D. T. (1958). "Balavignus and the Rebirth of Sanitation." In *Magic, Myth and Medicine* (p. 58), https://1ref.us/1c4 (accessed Sept. 23, 2020).

[18]Ibid.

[19]Dankenbring, William. "Bible Laws: The Foundation of Good Health," Herbert W. Armstrong Library, https://1ref.us/1c5 (accessed August 19, 2020).

[20]*8 Laws to a Better, Longer Life* (DVD), https://1ref.us/1c6 (accessed August 19, 2020).

Longer and Happier!"[21] I use this booklet in my ministry and encourage others to do so as well. As a lifestyle coach and drug and alcohol prevention educator, my hope is to help others implement these tools to life-saving methods to achieve optimal health.

1. Good News Then: in 1909 Mrs. Ellen G. White wrote a book called *The Ministry of Healing*. In the chapter titled "The Use of Remedies" she states principles with which to treat sickness. The include "The Diet-Cure," "Rest," "The Use of Water," "Benefits of Exercise," and finally, "Strictly temperate habits, combined with proper exercise, would ensure both mental and physical vigor, and would give power of endurance to all brain workers."[22]

2. Good News Now: The above five principles mentioned from Mrs. White are even more expertly expressed in the acronym NEWSTART and the enlightening materials mentioned previously which will help you live your best and healthiest life!

As a lifestyle coach and drug and alcohol prevention educator, I use the above principles to teach others to follow these lifesaving methods to achieve optimal health. The below points are taken from the "8 Laws to a Better and Longer Life" video:

N—**Nutrition:** God's original diet was a plant-based diet.

E—**Exercise:** A great way is walking in nature at least 2 miles/day or 30 minutes/day (best).

W—**Water:** Drink 6–8 glasses of water each day. Our body is mostly water and we should only be drinking water or fruit juice—not soda pop or other sugary drinks. Water is also essential on the outside of you to help fight the CoVid-19 virus. This is not only washing hands but using hydrotherapy to fight disease.[23] Hydrotherapy WORKS!

S—**Sunlight:** Spend at least 30 minutes/day outdoors. Take precautions to not burn in the sun.

T—**Temperance:** No alcohol period!!! No tobacco period!!! Or street drugs!!! MOTTO: Abstinence in what is bad and moderation in what is good.

A—**Air:** Do deep breathing exercises 3–5 times daily. Breathe in deeply and hold and then let the air our slowly. The result is that the toxins in the

---

[21]"Light Up Your Life!" by Health Expo Resources, https://1ref.us/1c7 (accessed August 19, 2020).
[22]White, Ellen. *The Ministry of Healing*, pp. 235–238 (https://1ref.us/1c8, accessed August 19, 2020).
[23]COVID-19 update 46, MedCram.com, https://1ref.us/1c9 (accessed Jun. 28, 2020).

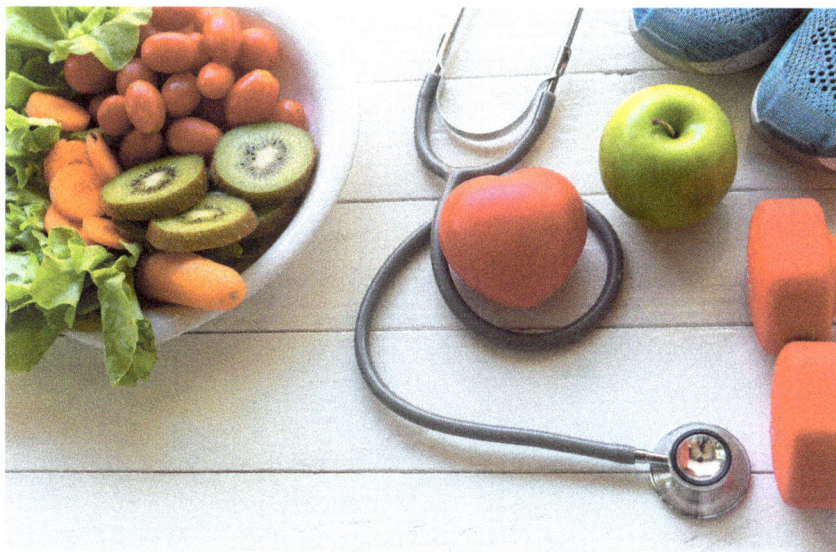

lungs clear out and you feel relaxed. This is best to do out-of-doors where the air is charged by a creek of water or near trees. Also, have fresh air coming into your bedroom through an open window.

R—Rest: Sleep for 6–8 hours each night. The best sleep happens before midnight. In fact, the ratio is every 1 hour of sleep before midnight is worth 2 hours or sleep versus 1 hour after midnight. Go to bed without anger and be at peace with all—including God. As scripture says, "Don't get so angry that you sin. Don't go to bed angry" (Eph. 4:26, CEV), Forgive others and go to bed in peace.

Additionally, in Genesis 2:1–3 we see Jesus is our Creator.[24] In creating us and our world, Jesus gave us the wonderful gift of REST. He blessed and sanctified the seventh day and made it Holy to worship Him as our Creator. He wants us to take this time to recover and reflect. This 24-hour period starts at sunset Friday (Lev. 23:32) and ends on Saturday night at sunset. This 24-hour "time out" from our very busy life of work gives us a mini-vacation each and every week to connect with Jesus and worship Him, have family time, and do as Jesus did by helping others. The end effect is to be refreshed and free of worrying about producing or accomplishing anything.

NOTE: My career and past life came to a sudden end because of NO Sabbath work. On God's special day I took His command found in Exodus 20: 6–11 to mean me. I gave up a career and the six years it took to acquire a master of arts degree and a full-time, good-paying job to follow God's

---

[24]See John 1:1–3.

9

command. QUESTION: Did God let me down? ANSWER: Absolutely NOT!!! God put me to work for Him and I served thousands of teens as a drug and alcohol educator. Was I qualified to teach the teens on this subject? The answer is 100% YES. I smoked, drank like a fish, and smoked marijuana in college. After conquering these demons with His help, for 28 years God blessed me in this education effort. My greatest wish is to see many of these youth in the Kingdom.

> *So, was it worth making a decision to honor God by keeping His seventh-day, holy Sabbath? Absolutely YES!*

So, was it worth making a decision to honor God by keeping His seventh-day, holy Sabbath? Absolutely YES! I spent time as a boy going into nature with my parents to national parks, beaches, day trips to the mountains, all to commune with the God of nature. Friends, this gave me a relief from the world and deeply blessed me in the days ahead.

T—**Trust in God:** When we read God's Word, His Holy Bible, we get to see His loving character. Per 2 Corinthians 1:20, His word is always yes and amen.[25] His promises are true and the more you walk with Him daily and meditate on Him, the closer you come to Him. His promises are always true. How "exceedingly great and precious promises" they are![26] Claim them by faith and stand on them. I have done this many times whether it be financial need or any personal disaster that has come my way. As the song goes "Tis so sweet to trust in Jesus." Prayer is so sweet also. Prayer is talking to Jesus, our best Friend, and listening to Him in His Word. What a blessing to do this each day! If we do so, a close relationship develops. The net result is inner peace when our world turns upside down.

Friends, these eight natural remedies, if all practiced daily, will boost your immune system. Couple this with a spirit of gratitude and daily service to others and you will have the best advantage you can to face all life's trials. The bottom line, as Proverbs 17:22 says, "A merry heart doeth good like a medicine." Also, service is what God made for us to help others, thus taking our minds off self. I live in the country in West Virginia and having good close neighbors is a must. We have the life and ability to do what the old frontier folks knew best... to depend on others.

Further, to help boost our immune system we must be "putting the best fuel" into our bodies. This would be having a daily balance of fruits, nuts, and grains, plus vegetables. This practice gives us all the vitamins and

---

[25]"For no matter how many promises God has made, they are "Yes" in Christ. And so through him the "Amen" is spoken by us to the glory of God" (NIV).
[26]2 Peter 1:4 (NKJV).

minerals our body needs. I spoke with Dr. John Westerdahl (of the Carter Report) on the phone about what foods can be called "Superfoods." I have included this list at the back of the book in the section titled "Super Food to Keep One in Optimal Health."

I now will take you back to how obeying God's health laws helped mankind. As mentioned, by following these laws found in the Old Testament of the Bible, the Jewish people have truly been helped during major health situations. But alas, it seems that our memories are short. By the 1800s we can observe a total breakdown in keeping the health laws and not until 1863 did we again see God's health laws revisited in America. In the 1900s things began to change. According to George Will, a syndicated national writer, "This is about when medicine at last began to do better than harm. Currently 37% of all deaths were from infectious diseases. In 2020 it is now 2%."[27] As you can see, as medicine has advanced, so has our knowledge of infection disease. Unfortunately, we have entered a period where our lifestyle choices directly influence mortality.

According to the latest data (2020), the worst lifestyle killers are:

1. Lung cancer
2. Coronary artery diseases
3. AIDS (acquired immunodeficiency syndrome) and HIV (human immunodeficiency virus) which damage the immunes system and interferes with the body's ability to fight disease.
4. Violence
5. Substance abuse
6. Type 2 diabetes (adult-onset)/obesity and other known to-be-at-risk behaviors.[28]

So, with 80% of all deaths being directly linked to our lifestyle, what can we do to live a healthy, productive, and long-lasting life? VERY simply follow God's health laws/plan. Follow what is referred to as NEWSTART (mentioned previously), developed by the Weimar Institute located in California. Today the proof of the efficacy of this lifestyle is found in Loma Linda, California. Around the world there are five area known as "Blue Zones," where people most often live to the age of 100+ with little cancer, heart problems, or diabetes. Loma Linda is one of these Blue Zones. The Seventh-day Adventists that live in this location live well beyond 100 and are in top health. Many go to the gym, swim, jog, and even drive when past 100 years of age.

---

[27]George F. Will, "And Enlightening Lesson from Nature," *The Exponent Telegram,* March 19, 2020.
[28]Ibid.

According to The University of Southern California, we can live to be 120—not the average age in America of 78.[29] So, again, if you want to live a long and productive life, follow God's health plan for optimal health!

I hope that you all have enjoyed this chapter on the history of America's health environment. As we move to Chapter 2, entitled "Life Trials," I would like to first see how much you have learned from Chapter 1. So, take out your pen or pencil and fill in the worksheet below.

Worksheet: USA Health

1. What were some of the standard medical treatments in the 1800s?

   _____

   _____

   Were they good? or bad? Explain:

   _____

   _____

2. God blessed Ellen G. White with a health vision in1863. Was this for mankind's best interest? or was this a waste of time? Explain:

   _____

   _____

3. In 1909 Ellen G. White wrote one of her many books, entitled *The Ministry of Healing*. Was this book cutting edge health instruction and timely? Yes or no? Explain:

   _____

   _____

4. The goal of this book is to show us that if we forget God's health laws, this can lead to disease. Do you agree? Why?

   _____

   _____

5. The book also lists lifestyle principles: nutrition, exercise, fresh air, rest, and trust in God. Can these principles boost one's immune system? Yes or No? Explain:

   _____

   _____

6. Between 1348 and 1351, Europe experienced the Black Plague. Did God's health principles slow it down among the Jewish people as

---

[29]https://1ref.us/1c9 (accessed Jun. 28, 2020).

they implemented the health laws of the Old Testament? Yes or No? Explain:

_____

_____

7. What is the age mankind can live to if we follow God's Health Laws?

_____

_____

8. Would you like to have a life goal to live that long and be in optimal health? Yes or No? Explain:

_____

_____

What do you need to do to reach that goal?

_____

_____

Chapter 2

Facing Life's Trials

As we all now face COVID-19 in 2020, we need to implement a major lifestyle change. Why??? Because we all will face major world problems going forward. This book discusses the facts as they now present themselves.

Before I jump into life's trials, let's look backward a little. In 1943, halfway through WW2, our country faced many problems. According to Mr. Charles Lane, a syndicated writer, "If economic privation deepens beyond a certain—still unknowable—point, so will the risks of cheating, hoarding, looting or worse. Even during World War II, home-front

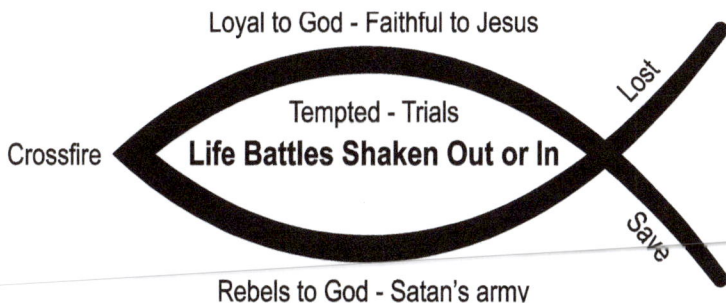

Loyal to God - Faithful to Jesus

Tempted - Trials
Life Battles Shaken Out or In

Crossfire

Lost

Save

Rebels to God - Satan's army

A Simple Overview of the Diagram is Helpful Now.

discipline began breaking down in 1943, which saw a wave of strikes and race riots."[30]

Could this happen again in America?

So, what happens if we have no hope and no loving Creator relationship in our life? Ultimately, stress and anxiety = fear= panic … all because one does not know and trust a loving God.

Trial Illustration

So, we now can see the worst of human behavior and how that lack of control and discipline lead to a multitude of problems. The number one question is how do we reverse those health destroying behaviors? I, personally, have found the answer in falling in love with God and His loving Son and trust in:

His love = God-like behaviors. With God's help, as outlined in the diagram below of the Ichthus (fish) symbol,[31] we can see how trials in our life can directly benefit us. Now, using Daniel chapter 11, we can see the crossfire that all Christians are going through.

If we view the front of the fish, we see *crossfire* listed. Chapter 11 of Daniel show us that battles rage between the King of the South and the King of the North. But in real life, life's battle under temptation affects us all.

The middle of the diagram shows what can happen in our trials. We can be shaken out or in, depending on how we react. With God's help and our choice, we can be loyal to God and be faithful to Jesus. And the result is we are saved for His kingdom. The opposite is also true: if we rebel against any life situation, we are drawn to the evil one who seeks only to destroy us.[32] The net result it we become a rebel and join his army of evil, seeking to harm others. As we go on in time, before Jesus comes, we will see the crossfire happen more in our lives. I have seen this happen in my life many times. So be faithful to Jesus and when tempted, follow the counsel of James 4:7–8: "Submit yourselves therefore to God. Resist the devil, and he will flee from you. Draw nigh to God, and he will draw nigh to you."

WHAT A LIFE PROMISE … PLEASE HOLD ON TO IT AND GOD WILL GIVE YOU THE VICTORY.

How Can Trials Benefit Us?

So, how can life's trials really benefit us? They direct us to our Savior, our Creator God.

---

[30]Lane, Charles. "Amid Coronavirus Fear, Economics Can Offer Hope," *The Washington Post,* https://1ref.us/1ca (accessed July 13, 2020).
[31]"What Is the Ichthus?" by BibleStudy.Org, https://1ref.us/1cb (accessed July 13, 2020).
[32]1 Peter 5:7.

a. They wake us up to our need of a loving God in our lives. As per Matthew 25:1–10, there are ten virgins and five of them have no oil for their lamps. They are unprepared and in need of the light-giving, life-saving oil. When behold the bridegroom cometh the wise are ready to go into the marriage supper.

b. We need to see the times we live in are according to the prophet Daniel. Daniel 7:10 is the judgement time: "the judgment was set, and the books were opened." The time of the end, according to Daniel's prophecy, is the 1,260 years starting in AD 538 and ending in 1798 and the 2,300 years prophecy of the Sanctuary being cleansed in Daniel 8:14. This correlates to Revelation 14:6, 7 where the first angel proclaims that the judgement hour has come. So when was this? In 1844 the message was proclaimed by William Miller in the eastern United States.[33]

c. Peter says "the end of all things is at hand" (1 Peter 4:7) and "for the time is come that judgement must begin at the house of God" (1 Peter 4:17).

d. Our faith will be tried. "My brethren, count it all joy when ye fall into divers temptations; Knowing this, that the trying of your faith worketh patience" (James 1:2, 3), and before Jesus comes back, "Blessed is the man that endureth temptation: for when he is tried, he shall receive the crown of life, which the Lord hath promised to them that love him" (James 1:12). Revelation 22:12 says, "And, behold, I come quickly; and my reward is with me, to give every man according as his work shall be."" John 5:29 says "And shall come forth; they that have done good, unto the resurrection of life; and they that have done evil, unto the resurrection of damnation."

e. They help our faith grow so we will be loyal to God and all His Ten Commandments. You see, Jesus is our Creator, forming Adam and Eve with His own hands. John 1:1–3 clearly states that Jesus is the world's creator: "In the beginning was the Word, and the Word was with God, and the Word was God. The same was in the beginning with God. All things were made by him; and without him was not any thing made that was made." Being loyal to Jesus and obeying Him ensures we will be ready for His soon second coming.

Future Word Problems—Our Life Trials

FRIENDS, the biggest trial(s) will soon come upon all the world. In Matthew 24 the disciples ask Jesus, "Tell us, when shall these things be? and what shall be the sign of thy coming, and of the end of the world?" (vs. 3). Jesus responds with the signs of His coming:

1. Many will be misled: "Take heed that no man deceive you" (vs. 4).

---

[33]"William Miller: Tell the World," Seventh-day Adventist Church, https://1ref.us/1cc (accessed July 13, 2020).

2. Who will fool the masses? False Christs: "For many shall come in my name, saying, I am Christ, and shall deceive many" (vs. 5).
3. Violence will be rampant. "And ye shall hear of wars and rumors of wars: see that ye be not troubled: for all these things must come to pass, but the end is not yet" (vs. 6). How very true this is today! Patrick J. Buchanan[34] illustrates this for us in his article "In the Pandemic, It's Every Nation for Itself.". He says, "How the EU's nation-states are reacting to the corona-virus crisis brings to mind … "Every man for himself." … From Denmark to Slovakia, governments went into aggressive virus-fighting mode with border closings." He goes on to discuss the many countries "heeding the call of tribalism and nationalism … erecting borders between countries, inside their cities and neighborhoods, around their homes—to protect themselves from their neighbors, even from their own grandchildren."[35] Further, Jesus says these wars—inner and external—are not to end.

So, what comes along with wars?

a. Famines[36]
b. Pestilences[37]
c. Earthquakes[38]

Today we see all of these the world over. Basically, our world is dying and all cry out to be delivered as Romans 8:22 says: "For we know that the whole creation groaneth and travaileth in pain together until now."

I would like to suggest that all readers of this book watch Pastor Scott Christian's video series entitled "Planet in Distress,"[39] Scott clearly shows that our world will not last much longer. In Matthew 24:8 Jesus says these things are just the beginning of sorrows. Friends, our only safety is living in, and walking with, Jesus 24/7.

So, now our biggest help versus our biggest trials is for us to be in Christ. Let's look at some Bible promises to give us strength as we face this unprecedented time in Earth's history:

1. Romans 15:13: "Now the God of hope fill you with all joy and peace in believing, that ye may abound in hope, through the power of the Holy Ghost."

---

[34]Patrick Buchanan was an assistant and special consultant to U.S. presidents Nixon, Ford, and Reagan. He is also a prolific writer of books and opinion pieces.
[35]Buchanan, Patrick. "In a Pandemic, It's Every Nation for Itself," *The Joplin Globe,* https://1ref.us/1cd (accessed July 13, 2020).
[36]Five countries most at risk for famine in 2020, BBC News, https://1ref.us/1ce (accessed July 13, 2020).
[37]Locusts in Africa, NPR, https://1ref.us/1cf (accessed July 13, 2020).
[38]Earthquakes archive, https://1ref.us/1cg (accessed July 13, 2020).
[39]Part 1, "In the Beginning" (https://1ref.us/1ch, accessed July 13, 2020); Part 2, "A Matter of Character" (https://1ref.us/1ci, accessed July 13, 2020); Part 3, "How to Prepare" (https://1ref. us/1cj, accessed July 13, 2020).

2. 1 Corinthians 10:4: "For they drank of that spiritual Rock that followed them: and that Rock was Christ."
3. 2 Corinthians 1:4: "Who comforteth us in all our tribulation, that we may be able to comfort them which are in any trouble."
4. 2 Corinthians 12:9: "My grace is sufficient for thee: for my strength is made perfect in weakness."
5. 2 Timothy 1:7: "For God hath not given us the spirit of fear; but of power, and of love, and of a sound mind."
6. We also need to be temperate in all things to hear God speak to us. Both 1 Corinthians 9:25 and 1 Peter 5:8 tell us to be temperate and sober. WHY? God's only method to speak to us is through our conscience. This is located in our pre-frontal lobe in the brain. If we live an intemperate life using alcohol, tobacco, street drugs, or any other thing that leads to addiction, we shut off the ability of the Holy Spirit to speak to us. Therefore, we must remember that our bodies are not our own. In 1 Corinthians 6:19 it says that "your body is the temple of the Holy Ghost." And Peter says in 2 Peter 1:6, "And to knowledge temperance; and to temperance patience; and to patience godliness.".

Put simply, if we live a temperate life we can see clearly the difference between what is right or wrong. When we make the positive biblical choice, we are blessed. Our minds are the battleground between God-like principles in His Word and Satan's goal to get us to rebel against God and be a part of his army (see previous Ichthus diagram). Why go toward Satan's ground when we have heaven to win and be with Jesus for eternity as stated in John14:1–3. So as the crossfire tightens on all the world, let's be drawn to God's Word when tempted and resist the devil as James 4:7, 8 says.

Trials Worksheet

1. Trials of life can make us or break us!
Yes or No? Explain:
_____
_____

2. How can our trails benefit us?
_____
_____

3. Our character either shines in major life trails or is crushed.
Yes or No? Explain:
_____
_____

4. What is a good character seen by all?

_____

_____

5. Each of us will soon face bigger life trials. Yes or No? Explain:

_____

_____

List some of them:

_____

_____

6. What will earth's condition look like soon according to Matthew 24:4–8?

_____

_____

7. Will there be more COVID-19 type diseases? Yes or No? Explain:

_____

_____

8. If we live a life of self-control, living with no alcohol, smoking and street drugs, will we be in much better health? Yes or No? Explain:

_____

_____

9. Also, if we live by God's health laws will we be able to see clearly what is best for our life? Yes or No? Explain:

_____

_____

On the flip side of this if we make wrong choices will that affect our health? How so?

_____

_____

Chapter 3

Intercessory Prayer

In the closing days of this world's history all Christians will be in a crossfire for the forces of evil will do all they can do to get God's children to reverse course and join Satan's army. The intense battle for the mind will necessitate a very deep prayer life. Our faith will be tried to the max. So, let's turn our attention to how prayer works by faith in God.

1. Prayer is speaking to God as we speak to our best friend, which is Jesus.
2. Prayer is how we communicate with God and Bible study is how God communicates with us. It is through the Holy Spirt that the Word of God was given to mankind. Thus, when we pray before we study God's Word, the Holy Spirit now is given permission to help us learn God's Word.
3. In our need to deal with anxiety and stresses of life, we must "Pray without ceasing" as the Apostle Paul says in 1 Thessalonians 5:17.

In what is called the Great Controversy between Satan and Christ for our souls, God is limited in what He can do for us. Because we have a will, only we can decide to put it on God's side. God cannot do this for us. It is Heaven's goal for us to merge our will with His goal. Heaven does not violate our will. We are free to place it with Satan or God.

Angel Help or Jesus Help

Defeat

Prayer

Life Battles Good and Evil

Victory

Power of Evil One and His Angels

This graphic shows us how intercessor prayer works.

1. I pray for a person named Sam to come to Christ;
2. Sam can accept the angel's help;
3. Or Sam can reject the angel's help.

We must realize that the power of evil (angels) demons truly exists. Their duty is to sink our life and destroy us. 1 Peter 5:8 says, "Be sober, be vigilant; because your adversary the devil, as a roaring lion, walketh about, seeking whom he may devour."

Job is an example of Satan's attempt to devour and destroy. In Job chapter 1, Satan is condemning God for giving Job everything, and says this is the only reason Job obeys. Satan says, "Hast not thou made an hedge about him, and about his house, and about all that he hath on every side? thou hast blessed the work of his hands, and his substance is increased in the land" (Job 1:10). God allows this hedge of protection to be withdrawn. In Job 2:7 we see how fast he was able to cause boils on Job. "So went Satan forth from the presence of the Lord, and smote Job with sore boils from the sole of his foot unto his crown." The immediate effects of Satan being able to inflict harm, with God's hedge lifted, was fast and to the point = destroy him if possible. Satan's attack resulted in ten of his family being killed and his property gone in one day. Satan's goal also was to inflect harm on God by harming Job. His wife says "curse God, and die" (2:9).

Friends, our only protection is the "hedge" stated in Job 1:10. God protects us by His angels and His obeyed Law. My prayer cry for help allows the angels to help me. "The angel of the Lord encampeth round about them that fear him, and delivereth them" (Ps. 34:7).

This happened in living color in the prophet Daniel's life. In Daniel 6:20 we find him cast into the lion's den. He spends the entire night resting with the peaceful lions! Just picture him resting in confidence in God's power to protect him. Prayer was an integral part of Daniel's life and led him to a deep trust in the safety his God provided him in His angels' arms.

So back to Daniel chapter 10.

1. Daniel has been praying for three weeks (10:3). Prayer has always been a part of his life, but now there is a very special need for intercessory prayer for the king to let God's people go home as the prophecy of the seventy years stated in Jeremiah 25:12: "And it shall come to pass when they seventy years are accomplished."
2. The angel Gabriel says that "thy words were heard" BUT...
3. In verse 13 he says, "The prince of the kingdom of Persia withstood me." Gabriel cannot get the King of Persia to soften his hard heart to let the Jews go back to Jerusalem to build the city.
4. What happens when the struggle between Satan hardening the king's heart now necessitates the "Chief Prince" to help? "But, lo, Michael, one of the chief princes, came to help me" (vs. 13). Jesus, the "Prince of Peace" (Isa. 9:6) now comes to help Gabriel influence the king.

How Prayer Works

As the battle for my soul lies in the power of my choice, Sam in the Ichthus diagram needs help. Our prayers allow God to send His angels to help him and to influence Sam to decide to be drawn to God. If no one prays for Sam, he could be lost unless circumstances in his life wake him up. These could be sickness, family death, divorce, financial losses, or many other things. At that time Sam might finally cry out for help. There's an old saying, "There is no atheists in a fox hole." In other words, when all hope is gone, faith gives you a place to hide in a war. The bottom line is we need to pray for others. One day in heaven we will see our prayers answered. My brother is a reformed alcoholic and drug addict. I spent much time praying for him over the years and he now is a serious Seventh-day Adventist Christian.

In summary, if no one prays for Sam, he does not receive Heaven's help if he is closed to receive it. In Ephesians 6:11 the Bible says, "Put on the whole armour of God." In earth's closing moments, in the very last seconds in our world's history, we all need to pray more, study more, and trust in God's promises completely.

Prayer Worksheet

1. According to the Ichthus (fish) diagram, when we pray who helps us?
_____
_____

2. Also, if a friend exerts a strong self-will, will they hear or relate to Heaven's help?
_____
_____

3. Is prayer like speaking to our best friend Jesus? Yes or No? Explain:
_____
_____

4. In what is called the "Great Controversy" between Jesus and Satan, can Satan move our will if we are open to it? Yes or No? Explain:
_____
_____

5. The flip side of this, can we be drawn to do God's will if others pray for us? Yes or No? Explain:
_____
_____

6. Did Job have a hedge around him? Yes or No? Explain:
_____
_____

7. When given freedom to hurt Job and his family, was this done very quickly? Yes or No? Explain:

_____

_____

8. In Earth's final moment, soon to come, before Jesus second coming, will we need to pray more? Yes or No? Explain:

_____

_____

9. Will trusting in God's promises in His Word will greatly benefit us? Yes or No? Explain:

_____

_____

My dear friends, if you are willing to go back to God's original diet for mankind, you will be blessed. God honors them that honor Him (1 Sam. 2:30).

God, through Moses, instructed the Hebrew nation by giving them His health laws in the Old Testament. While kept, they lived disease free. Exodus 15:26 tells us, "And said, If thou wilt diligently hearken to the voice of the Lord thy God, and wilt do that which is right in his sight, and wilt give ear to his commandments, and keep all his statutes, I will put none of these diseases upon thee, which I have brought upon the Egyptians: for I am the Lord that healeth thee."

My hope is that this simple blueprint you hold in your hands with help you and transform you and your family.

May I suggest you make things right with both God and your fellow mankind? The good news is Jesus will VERY soon come back for those who love Him, honor Him, and serve Him. So, go out and tell others what the tools found in this book have done for you.

Yours in Christ,
Brother Bruce

Super Foods to Keep One in Optimal Health

Compiled by Dr. John Westerdahl of Loma Linda University

1. ACAI BERRIES
2. ALMONDS
3. APPLES, ONLY ORGANIC
4. APRICOTS

5. BLUEBERRIES
6. BROCCOLI (FRESH PRODUCE)
7. CINNAMON. ORGANIC
8. CITRUS FRUITS, FRESH, NOT FROM CONCENTRATE AS THEY HAVE TOO MUCH SUGAR
9. CONCORD GRAPES, WHEN IN SEASON
10. FLAXSEED
11. GARLIC
12. GINGER
13. GOJI BERRIES
14. MANGO
15. MUSHROOMS (THEY UP THE IMMUNE SYSTEM)
16. OATS
17. PAPAYA
18. POMEGRANATE
19. SOYBEANS
20. TURMERIC
21. WALNUTS

Here are some other vegan superfoods to help you live your healthiest life:[40]

AVOCADO
SEEDS
BEETS
NUTS
NON-DAIRY MILK DRINKS

Remember that health benefits might vary, but God's foods are the core of wellness.

Boost Your Immune System the NEW START Way

Let's review how to boost your immune system the **NEW START** way:[41]

Nutrition—Concentrate on fruits, grains, nuts, and vegetables. Specifically, citrus fruits, carrot juice, garlic, and these herbs: golden seal, echinacea, olive leaf extract, oil of oregano.

Exercise—The lungs exhale toxins and as we perspire, toxins are eliminated through skin. Hormones are created which give a sense of well-being, thus stimulating the immune system.

Water—Drink one quart of warm water with juice of 1 lemon upon rising in the morning. Then drink about 1.5–2 quarts throughout the day. Drink water instead of other beverages. Shower once a day; take

[40]"17 Vegan Superfoods to Power You Through Life," https://1ref.us/1ck (accessed July 14, 2020).
[41]NEWSTART Lifestyle Program, https://1ref.us/1cl (accessed July 14, 2020).

hot/cold contrast showers or hot baths to enhance the immune system and fight off illness.

Sunshine—1 hour a day early morning or late afternoon. Vitamin D boosts the immune system.

Temperance—in all things; abstain from drugs, alcohol, and caffeine. Strive for balance in work, stimulating the mind through reading and sharing with others, and relaxation.

Air—Get plenty of fresh outdoor air. Outdoor exercise is ten times more effective at oxygenating the blood, which gives a tremendous boost to the immune system. Gardening, raking, and mowing are excellent. Sleep in a cool room with windows open.

Rest—Early to bed early (9 or 10 p.m.) and early to rise. This is the time for repair and restoration of our bodies and minds. Observe the Sabbath rest on the 7th day of every week. Break from your work by planning regular outings and annual vacations.

Trust in God—Cast your cares upon Him and give Him your worries. As you refuse to accept the burden of stress, your adrenals will be rejuvenated and your immune system strengthened. Develop an attitude of praise and gratitude! Study God's Word to strengthen your faith and trust in Him.

Reviews

"Bruce has made the important information and methods in this timely and relevant book easy to understand and to put into practice. I cannot imagine any thinking person who reads and puts into practice the principles found in this book not being benefitted themselves, and not being better equipped to help those whom they love and care about."

—Ron Clark, Former Field Representative Director for *Listen* and *Winner* magazines

"As a health professional and a firm believer of natural healing, I strongly agree that by following the Natural Laws of Health as Bruce clearly emphasized in his book is by far the best way to stay fit and healthy."

—Jean Wright, Registered Pharmacist and member of Philippine Pharmaceutical Association

"Bruce has put together a concise work that flows from his heart's experience. Bruce's short pamphlet comes along just as the world has been changed by the COVID 19 pandemic. This work prepares us for the pandemic and for the other events that will shake our world. His is a hopeful message."

—Dr. Art Calhoun, Medical Doctor

"Truly a very inspiring and informative narrative on how to reestablish a relationship God! This book is not only informative, but it also works as a Bible Study to discover what is God's 'Perfect Will for His Children!' The points highlighted really speak about reconnecting with our Creator, and this is something we must desperately do today!"

—Pastor Albert Rodriguez Senior Pastor in WV Mountain View Conference/my pastor

www.ingramcontent.com/pod-product-compliance
Lightning Source LLC
Chambersburg PA
CBHW041719090426

42739CB00018B/3480